State of Mind

by

Bernardino Pinna

To the memory of my parents, who raised
and educated me in the spirit
of liberated thinking
and freedom from prejudice,
for which I am eternally grateful.

First published in 2012

ISBN: 978-1-84289-016-5

Printed and bound in the UK

Published by Pomegranate Books, Bristol
www.pomegranatebooks.co.uk

Acknowledgements

I owe a special debt of thanks to my publisher, John Adler of Pomegranate Books, who, from the outset aided and assisted me in communicating what I wish to express, always endeavouring to understand my insights and putting his professionalism and cultural perceptions at my service. He has been an essential factor in bringing this book to fruition.

I also wish to express my deep appreciation of my partner Simona Mannozzi for her support and encouragement in the creation of this book, something she has done with great spirituality and love.

About the Author

Bernardino Pinna was born in Sardinia and came to live and work in the UK in 1997. In addition to writing on esoteric subjects he practices holistic medicine in Bristol, where he now lives.

Preface

Ever since I was a child, I have believed that every human being should express their sense of connection to the world by making a contribution to the well-being of humanity. I hope that through this small book, in which I have expressed my ideas on the nature of mind, I have in some small degree fulfilled this aim.

Bernardino Pinna

State of Mind

Introduction

What do we understand by the term 'state of mind'?

State of mind can be understood to be a holistic balance, holistic in the sense that it has a quality of completeness that is related to our surroundings as we perceive and experience them.

One's state of mind is affected by both positive and negative forces. When the part of our being connected to the world of emotions is not in a state of harmony, our vitality gets blocked and cannot find its true expression. This results in a sense of powerlessness because of the realisation that the element of balance is missing and it is the presence and manifestation of that sense of balance that creates the feeling of happiness in us. This is particularly relevant to the erotic element in our makeup.

Naturally, the way in which this occurs differs from one individual to another, yet the basic mechanism is the same in that it is governed by the dynamics of one's personal development.

For some, their superego is too dominant, and this has a negative impact; because the superego, being that part of the mind that is concerned with social morality and social acceptance, results in that individual being tormented by feelings of guilt and a stifling sense of taboo. As a consequence, they are unable to emancipate themselves from the power of the collective psyche of the society in which they exist, one that they often experience as overwhelming. This will result in the seed of their own individuality being unable to plant itself in their psyche. They feel crushed by the collective will and their own will is correspondingly negated.

Conversely, others suffer because, whilst their individual psyche has a sense of completeness, they are unable to enter properly into the world of the finite – or tangible reality as we might call it – since their individual psyche cannot find its place within the collective psyche of society at large.

There are, however, those who are able to reach a positive state of mind, because their individual psychology allows them to become connected to the collective psyche and so commune with their fellow human beings. Such individuals have been able to succeed in life on a personal, emotional and psychological level because they have been able to shape their individual psyche in a way that is governed and influenced by the path of their natural growth and development. In other words, their development has been organic and based on authentic, and genuine, individual needs, and not overly influenced by the mores and values of the majority.

Man
You are one
And never the same
In anyone's eyes.
You are one for yourself
And never the same for others.
Yet if the others are us
As we are the others,
Taken one by one,
Each one has an ego,
Similar, identical
Yet different, individual.
Looking at yourself
And in each one of the others
You see a reflection.

My understanding of the nature of thought basically breaks down into two different patterns of mental activity. They are quite distinct from one another yet need to be considered as part of the same reality, especially when they interact with one another. The first is what I call horizontal thinking, whereby humankind elaborates on what has been derived from the teaching of others. At the heart of horizontal thinking lies the superego, which filters experience through the prism of the knowledge and the education that has been imposed on us.

The second thought pattern is what I recognize as vertical thinking, which is derived from one's own individual consciousness. This thought pattern is based on the unique perceptions of each individual and is largely independent of received wisdom. It is what each individual succeeds in perceiving. It is something that goes beyond one's education and conditioning. So, one who engages in vertical thinking is able to gain the freedom of being able to develop their own individual reasoning and make it a central part of their growth as an individual. This in turn leads to wider awareness and provides the energy for spiritual development.

* * *

Seen from an holistic point of view, each person has seven senses. The so-called five senses that are commonly recognized are all physical: sight, touch, hearing, smell and taste. The sixth and seventh senses are thought and creative force. In other words, thought arises from experience.

As I have mentioned, the 'five senses' are bodily senses, in that they stem from the physical and are transmitted to the soul. The sixth and seventh senses are spiritual senses, which are transmitted to the physical body through interchange between the two. Together they create a union, which in turn leads to the formation of a holistic reality from which a new human entity is born.

To expand on the question of horizontal thinking, we can look at it as something that corresponds to the idea of the horizon, from which the term is indirectly derived. The horizon, in the sense that we think of it, is finite and limited. It is the end point of what we see. In terms of thinking, horizontal thinking is governed by what we have been taught or conditioned to believe. It is the state of dwelling in the conscious world of the exoteric – in other words, that which is comprehensible to the public, or people in general. It is, for the purposes of my argument, synonymous with a closed mind.

However, if we do not confine ourselves to a fixed position in our thinking, we can see that there is something beyond the horizon, in so far as that which is behind and alongside ourselves is also part of our horizon. In fact, the concept of the horizon is connected to the idea of a circle. When we look at the horizon in a seascape, for example, we can see that it is curved, not straight, because it follows the curvature of the earth and the earth is round, not flat, as it was perceived in former times. The

Earth is a sphere and is circular, and the circle is closed; it has no starting point and no end point; it is bounded but infinite. Correspondingly, mankind can develop from the starting point of horizontal thinking by expanding its vision and transcending its apparent limitations. The further it succeeds in doing this, the more it will understand the reality of the human condition that has been bestowed on it. For each individual, a great deal depends on developing one's sensitivity so that one can transcend the limitations imposed on our thought structure by the education and upbringing to which we have been subjected. What appears to be finite, in fact, has the potential of the infinite contained within it.

Vertical thinking is part of the same mechanism but,

conversely, it holds the potential for mankind to expand its consciousness by entering into the infinite nature of the circle and not be contained within its finite form. This is to enter the world of the esoteric, one that is the preserve of those who have chosen to expand their consciousness. As I have already pointed out, the exoteric is linked to the superego, the psychological mechanism that is rooted in conformity to the norms of social behaviour and function. On the contrary, the world of the esoteric is, by definition, transcendent and based on the principle of individual growth and development. To enter into the world of the esoteric is to use free will to liberate ourselves from the limitations and restrictions imposed by the superego. It is a journey that is powered by the desire to use this free will to engage in the kind of original and inspired thinking that offers the potential for spiritual growth. In other words, it is the way in which we can open our minds and begin to find answers for ourselves to the questions of reality and the world, based on our own personal, individual awareness and thereby transcending the locked room of the superego.

If we see horizontal and vertical thinking as two interconnected circles, the one pointing sideways and the other upwards, then we see a beginning in the form of a sphere. Conceptually, the universe has the qualities of a sphere, as do all the heavenly bodies that constitute it, and this is the dimension towards which mankind should be encouraged to move in its thinking, and the behaviour that accrues from its consciousness. The cosmos, itself, can be seen as a dimensional sphere in which the largest encloses the smallest – the galaxy encloses the planet, the planet encloses the atom, and so forth. And so the world corresponds to all of the dimensions, from the largest to the smallest, from the horizontal to the vertical, from the two-dimensional to the three-dimensional, and beyond.

* * *

As Einstein pointed out, the universe is composed of matter, which is actually energy. What appears to be solid and material on one level, is actually fluid and esoteric at a deeper level. Similarly, on the human plane, we have the world of the physical and the world of the spiritual, and both are profoundly related. As in the relationship of the world of Newtonian physics, where reality is solid and observable, and the world of quantum, which is concerned with particle physics, where everything is in a constant state of flux and movement, the two are inextricably bound up with one another and are not separate. They are different levels of the same reality, the one tangible and accessible to the physical senses, the other, to all intents and purposes, invisible but nonetheless there. In fact, the physical world is another dimension of the world of spirit, and is not separate from it.

Regarding the world of the physical and the world of the spiritual, mankind embraces the two and nowhere is this more manifest than in the world of thought, where we have ideas that are seated in the mechanism of the brain yet go far beyond its limitations as a physical entity. In fact the world of atomic energy, the mechanism that binds atoms together and governs their function, is connected to the phenomenon of the spiritual, as manifest in humanity in the holistic and esoteric sense. Physical matter is passive, whilst the spiritual, which is the energy of the soul, is active and capable of transcendental thought that can be manifested in action. It is like the energy that binds atoms together.

The key to this concept is thought, using the balance of horizontal and vertical thinking. The true starting point of the mechanism of thinking involves reaching the vertices, or furthest points of the horizontal and vertical, then going to their centres and expanding out, remembering the circle as the basic model to which one should relate this mechanism. Then one returns to the centres, and in so doing creates a circulation of thought that goes beyond its imposed restrictions. The more one is able to expand the vertices of one's thinking, both upwards, downwards and laterally, the more one approaches the state of an open mind, with all that that implies. The extent to which one can open one's mind is directly proportional to the extent to which one is able to approach the aforementioned vertices and then go back. In this way, the true reality of the world can begin to reveal itself, relative to the extent to which one has succeeded in traversing its dimensions. A human being, and mankind in general, is both the subject and object of this process at one and the same time.

Let us assume that a person has managed to initially form a perfect dimensional sphere in their thinking and has begun to move onto the corresponding dimensional sphere, in that they have begun to glimpse this other dimension in some small degree. This process leads naturally from the one to the other, with the effect that it expands the individual's capacity for perception, reasoning and thought. In time, this phenomenon will spread and begin to influence the thinking of others, and eventually mankind as a whole, gradually and increasingly. By facing that which is hidden and discovering the reality that lies beneath appearances, we can establish an individual starting point for personal growth. This is achieved through what I call the three dimensions of consciousness.

The first and lowest level is bound up with the ego and the gradual awareness of its presence and influence in our thinking. This where we begin to realise the 'me' in our relationship to 'us', or to the world in general.

In the second layer of consciousness, mankind changes its way of thinking, in that it causes its beliefs to be materialised, and these beliefs become the basis for its individual and collective behaviour. In other words, a new psychological reality emerges that influences the behaviour of mankind, so that perception and action become profoundly connected.

The fruition of these stages of psychological and spiritual development is the third dimension of consciousness, where the mind opens up and is able to see beyond the veil of appearances, where the true nature of causality becomes evident and deceptive appearances evaporate as a consequence. What we now have is a metamorphosis where thought evolves in line with the growth of perception and consciousness. As we know, thought changes in the light of awareness. This is the way in which mankind can progress and begin to move into a new dimension of reality, which has the power to change everything for the better.

* * *

This process of entering into new dimensions of thought does not always yield results automatically. To enter into a given dimension does not necessarily mean that you have mastered it, because it can still be full of shadows and dark, impenetrable elements. If this is the case with even one part of the whole, then one cannot shed light on the entire truth – the part that is beyond appearances – and so one cannot project compete consciousness onto the situation, and as a result one's sense of reality is inevitably incomplete. This diminished sense of consciousness has its own penalties in that there is an ever-present danger of becoming trapped into thinking that one's interpretation of an apparent reality is the true one when it is not, with the risk that one might become stranded in a state that can only be described as 'anti-consciousness'.

The sense of dimension in thought has yielded rich rewards throughout the development of humankind. This so-called penetration of the dimensions has enabled, from the earliest times, the discoveries that have taken the human race forward – such as the use of fire, the wheel, the application of the realisation that wood floats on water, the extraction of metals, and so forth. The very idea of technology, which aids the mastery of our environment, is rooted in this matter of the dimensions. In these matters, one thing leads to another. For example, the discovery of metals led to the ability to exploit and apply their different properties, such as ductility and pliability, enabling the creation of ploughshares and cutting implements. The application of the qualities and properties of fire, for example, enabled these processes to be further developed, contributing to the advance of civilisation. Advances in basic technology in the primitive, non-theoretical sense, gradually led to the extrapolation of the theory that underlies it, with the emergence of what we now know as science. Technology and science are, in reality, a progression, whereby discoveries are combined and interlinked, enabling new inventions and discovery. In other words, they are the product of holistic thought. It is purely due to holistic thought that breakthroughs in the application of observable reality are possible, and the application of memory and imagination is central to this. That is why one thing leads to another in technology and science. For example, in this way we have been able to build increasingly sophisticated weapons, to develop the wheel from the wooden form to the metallic, and so forth. The recognition that metals do not float on water had many early applications, such as the invention of the ship's anchor. Yet it was due to a leap forward, arising from conceptual or dimensional thinking, that scientists like the Englishman John Wilkinson recognised the principle of the displacement of water and was able to float his twenty-one-meter-long iron barge on the Severn River, thereby proving that metals can be made to float. His achievement was the product of transcending his psychological state and thereby opening up his mind. This was dimensional thinking in action, with the result that what the world thought impossible became possible, with countless benefits for humanity as a whole.

All this demonstrates the principle that when mankind is able to transcend its psychological barriers, the mind opens up progressively and increasingly. This, in turn, enables the improved flow of thought and the ability to gain control of the dimensions. What this teaches us is that the reality of the world is relational by nature; that everything is interconnected and that an open mind creates the potential to transcend the limitations of thought and move forward, through the means of perception, introspection, reasoning and creativity in terms of their true relationship to one another. Herein lies the source of the magic of the world of creative art.

* * *

There is something ultimately elusive about the deeper nature of the mind and its relationship to thought. In my understanding, it is a mistake to place too much emphasis on the mind and thought as a means of control, i.e. the source of the idea that our path to understanding the world, and reality in general, is purely through reason and observation. Today, this is a very prevalent idea, but one that I would describe as material thinking. To me, the mind is more in the nature of a kind of invisible valve; the more this valve is opened, the more it allows thought to flow, with all its magical energy. In other words, more important than forcing the mind to function, which is actually a potentially stressful activity, is the idea of 'allowing' it to function. By opening up the mind in this way, and carefully focusing its activity rather than trammeling it, we can move from introspection to abstraction and, from this base, generate the process of organic reasoning which in turn leads to creativity. The mind can just as easily be a means of blocking the flow of creativity as a means of channelling it.

In relation to thought, the mind is none other than the key that allows each individual to find a state of equilibrium with their perception and awareness of reality. It enables this mechanism, in that it allows the process to take place, because it is only thought, by focusing attention, which enables reasoning. In other words, reason needs to be applied to experience, and the purer, more open, and truthful the experience, the richer the material to which reason can be applied. In other words, reasoning is a tool, and not a prime mover. This recognition is at the heart of true creativity.

So, the answer to the question, 'what is thought?' is, in my view, that thought arises from the psyche – the thinking energy of the soul, its spirit.

* * *

The psyche is a source of energy that can cause a given reality to materialise; that is within the limits of what is possible, vis-à-vis cause and effect. When someone seeks to carry out a project where he wants or needs to involve others, it cannot be fulfilled if this person lacks a harmonious relationship with all who are within the relationship as a whole. The law of human relativity is of fundamental importance here, as balance is required in relationships with other people, or indeed anything else involved in that relationship. The importance of intelligence is, with its ability to balance the possibilities of causal effects, naturally of paramount importance, and the capacity for success will be directly proportional to one's ability to exploit possible solutions.

Inevitably, in any project that involves others, the potential for success will also be governed by the ability to involve the others, even if, in theory, it has been possible to find all the necessary solutions. Yet, in practical terms, when there is no collaboration with others, it will not be possible to bring the project to fruition.

This simple and seemingly obvious recognition demonstrates how all that exists within our personal and individual space is, in fact, related to the reality around us, in its entirety. No matter how far the extent of intelligent willpower might be able to bring about the metamorphosis of consciousness, it is not possible, with our willpower on its own, to create that same metamorphosis of others' willpower without their consent and approval. Similarly, we can also see how the will of others can obstruct or neutralise the willpower and creativity of an individual, or another group, because we are all interrelated.

* * *

How can mankind protect itself from this negative aspect of human relations? I believe that the only clear solution is to develop an understanding of how these negative mental fields operate and how they can be neutralised, since the psyche is the root from which the willpower of the spirit is able to transform into psychic energy, an energy that transcends the normal limitations of material reality.

In order for spirituality to express its power, it must first be transformed into energy, and it is thanks to the psyche that this can take place, as it has the quality to transform the force that seeks to impose itself on us, against our better interests, into energy, which has a healing and regenerative quality. With this energy we can become masters of our fate, neutralising the power of negative relationships by creating a field of energy around us, which has the potential to transform the negative into something positive.

A fundamental requirement in being able to start the process that enacts this neutralisation is self-esteem. In order to develop self-esteem, we need to feel comfortable with ourselves, which means concerning ourselves with that which we like and admire – those things that genuinely interest us – and avoiding focusing on those things we do not like. It is especially important not to become subject to resentment, because, if we dwell on negative thoughts, we are only wasting our energies uselessly and, even worse, generating a reality that we do not want or need, as opposed to that which we are truly seeking. We should only concentrate on positive things; things that are able to furnish our will with intelligence; all those things that constitute our true personality and lead us towards a state of constant, ongoing spiritual growth. When we come up against limits, we only have to open our minds further for the flow of thought to focus within the union of horizontal and vertical thinking, widening horizons and reaching new vertices, in order to find new solutions. Our state of mind is the holistic equilibrium that grows out of our perceptions and vision. Because it is so closely linked to positive and negative forces, we must only follow the kinds of thoughts that bring us a sense of happiness.

Furthermore, state of mind is the alarm that tells us whether our thoughts are negative or positive. If our state of mind is negative, and we are having negative thoughts, we only have to return to a state of positive thinking, with the positive state of mind that follows on from this, and a solution is found. In order to achieve good results, clearly we must never lose self-esteem. It is through dwelling on things that are of no genuine interest to us, or remaining trapped by the negative force of resentment, that the psyche will cause these negative aspects to materialise and manifest themselves.

Thought takes no notice of what we want or do not want. It materialises precisely that which we think. From this simple truth, we can begin to realise how vitally important it is to think with intelligence and wisdom, because mankind basically becomes what it thinks.

For example, there are those who believe it right to confront the will of others. Instead of seeking an alliance, whereby the forms of thought achieve cooperation and generate mutual respect, placing everyone in agreement, instead they seek out conflict as the only solution to their problems. This can never lead to a constructive life. It has to be understood that the world belongs to everyone. This is why it is necessary to be able to live alongside others without imposing our ideas on them, with each party simply respecting the ideas of the other and, at the same time, taking the opportunity to learn to appreciate others.

In the final analysis, experience holds the key to the meaning and purpose of life. It is through opening ourselves up to the experience and knowledge, both of other people and the world in general, that it is possible, through one's own sensibility and reasoning, correctly applied, to avoid falling into the kind of useless and potentially destructive utopias that have so characterised the history of humankind and with such unfortunate consequences.

* * *

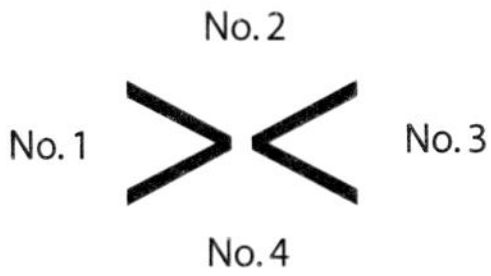

In this diagram, which I call the 'cosmic law of relativity', triangles nos. 1 and 3 represent positive force and negative force respectively, while nos. 2 and 4 are the neutral fields.

The negative force and the positive force mutually repel each other, whilst the neutral fields of no. 2 and no. 4 neutralise both the positive and the negative force. All of creation is linked to this law. In turn, this law is linked to the law of cosmic resonances, which states that when sounding a note and making it vibrate, through the cosmic law of vibrations, all the other notes will also vibrate similarly. For example, if we hang a guitar on the wall, whose strings are perfectly tuned, and take another guitar, also perfectly tuned, and make one of the strings on one of the guitars vibrate, through the law of cosmic resonances, the same note will also vibrate on the other guitar.

The whole universe is in a vibrational relationship, based on a scale of seven musical notes. The complete scale always ends with the repetition of the last end of the first note, which is made to vibrate, so that, if we start with *do,* it will be: *do, re, mi, fa, so, la, si, do*. Beginning with *re* it will be: *re, mi, fa, so, la, si, do, re,* and so on. Then, by using all the ¼ tones and ⅛ tones, and so forth, and at the same time sound the vibrations in different keys, we have at our disposal an infinite set of vibrational combinations. From this, one can imagine how much creativity and mutuality is available to mankind.

This is how the drawing demonstrates the way this phenomenon relates to mankind. The whole universe is energy and all this energy is ultimately in the form of vibration. Similarly, all of creation is the materialisation of thought, as is its continuous movement.

* * *

We can define primordial thinking as archaios, in the sense of absolute beginning, and sophia – absolute knowledge. This is archaic wisdom, the original wisdom, which, from the beginning of time, has materialised the reality of the world, providing its moral, spiritual and physical laws.

Mankind, itself, is also the materialisation of the intelligence arising from archaic knowledge, in which the laws of cosmic harmony have been instilled, and where it is both subject and object. Only archaios is object and not subject, in that everything derives from the origin of all things, and by His will. At the same time, everything is outside of Him, as He dominates all creation with His energy.

Yet creation can never be the equal of archaios, in that archaios circulates in creation with His energy, but the creation can never circulate in archaios, because archaios is only the manifestation of His being and the creation is the object, or purpose, of its being, and so is subject to archaios.

* * *

Archaic intelligence is specifically the ability to materialise reality according to its own inherent design. The principle of the movement of everything, as illustrated in the example of resonating notes, was created from the materialisation of archaic thought, in keeping with the quality of its aesthetic beauty. Beauty, in the original, archaic sense, expresses itself according to those fundamental laws that are instilled in it, according to a very specific design. Beauty is the manifestation of spiritual correspondence and harmony

Mankind is linked to this reality and, since mankind possesses a psychic energy able to materialise reality, it complies, collectively and individually, with the intrinsic intelligence inherent in that archaic law, which originally materialised the reality of the world.

In this way, we can see how, in reality, the rational intelligence that has materialised the principle of everything has done so according to an already instilled intelligence. Part of this is the instinct of preservation, which is given to all living forms so that they maintain the universally fundamental laws intact that gave them their very existence. This ensures that cosmic equilibrium is not altered and its design is left intact, on the basis that it has been archaically created. If we look inside ourselves, we will come to see this indisputable reality.

Examples of this include how life is created

spontaneously, according to its formative laws, a good example being the involuntary nervous system. Another is how the universe is underpinned by the laws of magnetic energy. We could go on endlessly.

Because of this all-embracing law, mankind has the possibility of materialisation only within the possibilities of cosmic movement and always according to the laws already inherent in cosmic reality – laws already materialised through the will of archaic intelligence.

The ability to float metals on water is none other than a discovery based on adherence to existing laws of physics. This means that mankind can engage with and exploit the reality of the world only in terms based on the discovery of its laws and the understanding of how to use them to its advantage. This relates both to physical matter and to the spiritual.

Ultimately, the assessment of the intelligence of mankind will be rooted, not only in the extent of its technological breakthroughs, but in both the physical and metaphysical – in mankind's ability to overcome the psychological state that threatens to block the capacity for maintaining an open mind. It should be recognised that mankind is not given the ability to create, but only that of being creative, in that it possesses the magic of the world of creative art – something inherent that can manifest itself when it is allowed to do so, and not something, as commonly believed, that is mentally generated – a so-called 'prime-mover'. When Descartes stated 'Je pense donc je suis', ('I think, therefore I am'), he failed to recognise that reasoning is a tool that is in the service of a deeper, intuitive, and spiritual reality.

The magic of creative art can only be developed when mankind, through the medium of an open mind, succeeds in overcoming the psychological state that would otherwise prevent its expression. Psychology is no more than a way of thinking. It is the manifestation of a scheme of reality we have constructed, in which we have created a specific and bound entity. One example is ideology, where individuals and groups have constructed an idea of something that involves shutting off their minds to a way of seeing and believing, which in reality is inherent within reality itself. Religion is often a vision of life derived from a notion of human behaviour whereby mankind derives its sense of identity from the concept of 'me' and 'us', whereas me and us, or the individual and the collective, is actually a reductionist view of a transcendental reality. In this way, the mind remains closed, stuck in a reality which mankind has materialised at a collective level, resulting in men fighting against each other, seeing in those of another, opposing ideology or religion, an enemy to be fought and destroyed.

This is the human psychological mechanism, which results from minds being closed off, producing thoughts of how one's individual or collective vision is the only correct path to follow.

Furthermore, this psychological mechanism invites

the power instinct, resulting in the subordination of people and keeping them enslaved to the superego. This superego does not permit the state of an open mind that is necessary for creating the flow and kind of thought essential to overcoming this behavioural, psychological barrier.

It should not be forgotten that people become what they think. However, a more serious problem arises when people think according to other people's imposed ideas, that accrue from teaching, in the form of culture, tradition and beliefs. This is how a reality gets materialised through horizontal thinking alone; a mechanism of human thought that applies to both religious and political ideology.

Perhaps the most dramatic examples of what results

from this kind of thinking are communism, fascism and nationalism in general, together with all forms of racism in religious and political movements. This psychological mechanism produces the notion that difference is seen as the enemy. Only with an open mind is it possible to combine horizontal and vertical thinking to produce dimensional thinking, which will lead people to a positive engagement and the gaining of new experiences in order to achieve spiritual growth. Through this development, people are able to gain access to awareness of the reality of the world beyond them, increasingly mastering dimensional realities and moving forward, through their own consciousness, towards the development of their individuality and growth.

What is so deeply needed is the enrichment of the community, which takes us ever higher towards a more elevated spiritual knowledge, to be able to materialise reality according to the design underlying it, and according to our will, as derived from the growth of personal wisdom.

In evolving our own spirituality, our personal creative potential can be realised through the expression of aesthetic beauty. This emerges from individual talent founded on true free will, which, in turn, is derived from our destiny based on the principle of archaic design.

We can conclude from this that the mechanism of dimensional thinking is none other than the extension in space of horizontal and vertical thinking, in the dimensions of width, length and height. This is what is really meant by being 'broad-minded'. In this way, we are able to expand and develop according to all possible movement of this spatial/spiritual reality. Through the wisdom achieved, this pathway will lead to progress into a new dimension of thought and sensibility that leads to an enlightenment, that opens up to us every possible combination, by which it is then possible, through personal talent, to manifest creativity in every dimension.

* * *

Returning to the structure of the cosmic law of relativity and the reality of the world that it underlies, it consists, in the symbolic sense, of a series of spheres of different dimensions, in which the largest encloses all the smaller ones. As I mentioned earlier, I have an image of eight dimensional spheres, which corresponds to the musical scale composed of seven notes. Imagine the centre of the spheres starting from the smallest, where the vertices that form the bases of triangles, representing the negative, the positive and neutral fields according to the cosmic law of relativity, lead off. The triangles of the positive and the negative arrive as far as the sphere of the seventh dimension but do not reach the eighth. Unlike the neutral fields, of which the eighth dimension only exists as part of the reality of the neutral field, it cannot penetrate any of the corners, either of the positive or of the negative, since it is solely a dimension of the neutral field. Consequently, these neutral fields, which reach out into every dimension, are none other than the energy that sustains cosmic reality.

The entire reality of the creation cannot go beyond the seventh dimension because, without the possibility of the eighth dimension making its use of the positive and negative fields, they would be neutralised permanently. I therefore conclude that the maximum possible degree of progression for mankind is to reach the seventh dimension.

In order to reach the seventh dimension, mankind must first master all the others, starting with the smallest. The question is, how can this be attained? Whilst it is definitely not easy to achieve, we will get there, step by step. As I mentioned previously, thought has its own circulation, in a sense not unlike the circulation of the blood. Just as the blood brings oxygen and nutrition to the body, so the neutral fields act in a way that is analogous to lymphatic circulation, complete with its antibodies.

Through the five bodily senses, mankind transmits the qualities of physical experience to the soul. Yet, spiritual growth takes this a step further, through the two additional faculties of reasoning and what is known as the sixth sense – the psychic. There is also a seventh sense, which, through the agency of universal psychic force and reason, is able to manifest the reality of the world of ideas. This, in other words, is the creative energy of dimensional thinking, without which mankind cannot be creative in its interaction with the world. This is because the reality of the world has already been created, complete with its potential for movement and causal effect. Yet it can materialise the reality of ideas through the infinite possibilities presented by movement, which is the foundation of progress. This is one of the phases of circulation in thought.

It is through the channel of archaic intelligence that ideas have materialised and have become a tangible reality, with all the inherent possibilities of progress. Indeed, mankind, itself, is the materialisation of an idea. Even if, according to evolutionists, mankind evolved from lower forms physically, the idea of man was there from the beginning, the underlying intelligence of this materialised idea is made possible by the two senses of the soul: the psyche, which transforms force into energy with which the sixth sense reasons, and the seventh sense, which materialises the idea. From this dynamic emerges the magic of the world of creative art.

Mankind is able to organise reality as an ongoing, continuous progression through the medium of psychic intelligence, combined with individual aesthetic sensibility. Thought, arising from the source of cosmic reality, evolves into an idea and, in turn, the idea returns to the source.

In this way, we can deduce that intelligence is an innate force in the universe, which nourishes the higher sensibility of mankind in the way that blood nourishes the physical body – it is a spiritual life force – whilst the neutral fields are like the system of lymphatic circulation with its antibodies, as was explained previously. The whole reality of the universe, and everything in it, is rooted in the sense of relationship, and relationship is aligned to energy. This energy is none other than vibration. As a consequence, mankind is subject to the law of cosmic vibration, which can be either resonant (harmonious) or dissonant.

* * *

Mankind has two important scales of values in its quest to master dimensional thought. The first is rooted in the realisation of individual value, while the other relates to collective value – what one might loosely call the social. Both are closely linked to feelings, which can be positive, giving us a sense of love, self-esteem, self-respect and respect for others; or, conversely, they can be negative, causing the opposite feeling – resentment, leading to hatred, intolerance and a lack of both esteem and respect for oneself and for others. Through positive feeling, we can find the harmony of love – of the 'me' within 'you', reaching completeness in the sense of 'us'. With negative feeling, there can never be harmony in the ego and the 'you' can never be joined to the 'us', resulting in a lack of completeness.

We can see another perspective to this phenomenon in man's relationship to animals. With animals, we do not relate to them on a strictly verbal level of communication, i.e. communication is not based on the meanings of words. Instead, it is based on emotions and sensations. In other words, it is a relationship of mental communication in the non-reasoning sense. When feelings are created between a man and an animal, they generate a sense of trust, respect and esteem, which can enable a positive relationship to emerge, based on mutual love. On the contrary, when emotions create a sense of mistrust, neither esteem nor confidence will be generated, so mutual affection cannot be created. Consequently, neither friendship nor an alliance will result.

Regarding the relationship between mankind and the plant and mineral world, humans will neither have a positive nor negative psychic relationship with these two worlds, but, instead, will be subject to their causal effect on the basis of the attitude and behaviour shown to them. This is due to the fact that we are connected to these worlds through the equilibrium of the animal sphere, which, although it is not at the same level as the human, is nonetheless every bit as real and consequential. We only have to think of oxygen, something that is invisible yet is a vital element of nourishment, and climate, which envelops and affects us profoundly. Yet we should also reflect on the fact that plants and minerals are beneficial to man on a level that goes beyond the physical, by virtue of the type of vibrations they emanate and through which we are interconnected.

* * *

Clearly we must ask ourselves how a man, who nowadays has an average lifespan of 75 to 80 years, can, in this brief space of time, master all the dimensions of thinking that are necessary for a meaningful and truthful life?

For the most part, mankind has a vision of life that is based on an inculcated idea – that once we die we will pass into the afterlife with the soul entering into a spiritual dimension. This belief system is the product of the kind of religious ideas that have created a psychological state whose manner of thinking is limited and fixed. As mankind develops in the future through new generations, its thinking will evolve towards a system that becomes increasingly able to penetrate the truth of things.

My ideas on thought and the nature of reality, as expressed in this book, have led me to a belief in the principle of reincarnation. With reincarnation, where the soul grows and develops in stages through the experience of inhabiting new bodies in succeeding lives, it is through the lessons of the previous life, as they are taken forward and built upon, that progress is made possible. Step by step, we are able to move forward, building upon the knowledge gained to create an awareness of the truth of human reality as it really is, together with its relationship to reality as a whole.

To my way of thinking, when the physical body dies, it passes into another dimension. The physical body lives in a holistic reality, where the five senses enable the human entity to experience physical reality. This emanates from the point of view of horizontal thought, complete with physical sensation and the reality that implies.

Through vertical thinking, we are able to exercise the powers of deduction and the gaining of experience, complete with human sensibility, the powers of soul perception and the ability to materialise ideas.

With death where we pass into another dimension, the situation is, in a sense, reversed, in that it is no longer the body which has a vision of the horizon but instead the soul, now that it has been released from the body. Through the wisdom gained from the experiences received via the earthly, holistic state of being, the soul is able to expand into a cosmic dimension of experience, through the application of its improved and broadened knowledge of physics and metaphysics, together with their interaction and causal effects. In this way, the human entity that survives death is able, through the mechanism of reincarnation, to reverse its earlier state of being and all that arose from it, by choosing not only a new body, but a new more advanced brain that will allow it to manifest psychic energy in the best possible way, once the opportunity to reincarnate has presented itself.

This cycle of reincarnations can only end when the wisdom has been gained that will enable the creation of a physical body, albeit one whose physical dimension is minimal, whose qualities enable it to become immortal. From this state comes the kind of perfection that allows the soul to enter into a spiritual, holistic relationship with all of reality. No longer will mankind be bound by that psychological/mental relationship, which prevents the possibility of its full expression in the form of psychic energy. So this new state of being allows the individual to become master of himself with self-knowledge and thus able to conquer all the seven dimensions of sense.

Through transcending this psychological state, we will be able to overcome the stultifying feelings of resentment in the future, and by resentment I mean the reverse sentiment to love, which is an open state of feeling.

Only by overcoming resentment is it possible to reach the true sense and value of universal love, which actually sustains the universe. The combining of 'me' and 'you' in 'us' in the complete sense, is the only way of creating the harmony of universal love in perfect symbiosis. With this, mankind can no longer continue to be a victim of itself, due to the negative dissonances which it has created itself through a deficient psychological state of being; one that prevents the opening of the mind and its progression towards that potential by which it can achieve mastery of the seven dimensions, and, in so doing, fulfil its destiny.

One's state of mind must constantly be kept under review and analysed in order to understand the kind of mental processes that are involved in one's relationship, both to others and to oneself. We should never lose sight of the law of cosmic resonances, which vibrate together and are the basis for the sense of affinity and mutuality with others. By being watchful and carefully analysing one's state of mind, it is possible to understand what mental processes are brought into play in relationships with others and make corrections accordingly, where necessary.

Knowing how to communicate is a human necessity, and in order to do this mankind needs a correspondence of ideas, otherwise communication is impossible. Those who wish to communicate must be able to express themselves in relation to others, gaining their interest in the process, since the listener has to enter into a state of open mental contact with the person seeking to communicate and a process of attunement is needed. This is the basis for open-minded dialogue and communication on a mutual basis, where thoughts are on the same vibrational wavelength. We use the colloquialisms, 'being on the same wavelength' or 'picking up another's vibes'. According to the law of cosmic vibration, we can see that this is literally true.

When men act in concert with one another, it is much easier to find, through collaboration, the strength to progress one's own destiny. However, when this potentiality is undermined, a man gets isolated and consequently weaker, since the lack of consensus, in respect of his values, means he faces adversity. In this situation, man must not allow himself to fall victim to negative feelings as this creates resentment. As a consequence of this resentment, negative vibrations are created according to the law of cosmic resonances. It is not difficult to imagine how much tension can be materialised by such a mental state.

For this reason, intelligent wisdom is required, opening up the mind and using both horizontal and vertical thinking in conjunction with one another, i.e. dimensional thinking. Using the dynamics of the cosmic law of relativity, one needs to enter into a neutral field of thinking and so allow oneself to be guided by a positive state of mind. If, after one has neutralised the negativity, materialised new solutions by means of dimensional thinking, and then returned to the way of the positive force, one can never be trapped in a negative field.

Likewise, we must never allow ourselves to be imprisoned, by believing that, because we are in a neutral field, we are safe. This is because, in the act of surrendering to a neutral field, our own willpower is also neutralised.

The only viable way is that of positive action and the neutral field must only be used solely and exclusively for neutralising the negative. This can give us the time and space necessary to bring about a new positive solution, because mankind has the resource of the magical power of the world of creative art in order to master his destiny, and the way to that objective is through mastering, and putting into operation, the seven dimensional spheres.

* * *

Mankind does not have the power to create things in the original cosmic dimension, since mankind is itself part of creation materialised. It does however, have power, derived from the magical world of creative art, to which its destiny is linked. So, by gaining consciousness of all seven dimensions, mankind will no longer be a prisoner of its own ignorance and will consequently be able to exercise its dominion in the world. with all the divine joy, blessing and beauty that arises from this, experiencing in the most complete happiness the reality of the world.

Mankind will discover true freedom of choice in the

awareness of its own will. This, in turn, will guide it so as not to submit to any negative feelings. As a consequence, it will have overcome each and every psychological barrier, and live with the absolute love of the life given to it with awareness of self-knowledge and the knowledge and understanding of others. From the power of the world of creative art, mankind can materialise its inner nature, co-vibrating in perfect symbiosis and in complete harmony with all the things that have been given to it, together with life itself. When mankind has succeeded in overcoming the obstacles of negative psychological states, and once it has gained awareness of the seven dimensions, it will no longer be subject to resentment and all the negativity that implies.

I like to think that men will be like an orchestra, in which each one will vibrate in harmony with his fellows, according to his uniqueness and individual talent; an orchestra that will have the honour of having as its audience the eighth dimension, which will applaud each part of the entire orchestra, and so finally achieve the circulation of intelligence together with the circulation of the neutral fields of this universal body, thereby leading to a symbiosis of perfect harmony.

Postscript

I dedicate these thoughts to the value of aesthetics, as aesthetics is the embodiment of the beauty of humankind. At the same time, I would like to acknowledge the significance of *archaios*, which, as well as life, has given us aesthetics as both an intrinsic and extrinsic quality of life, and so forming the essence of the attraction of life itself.

Bernardino Pinna, 2012

9781842890165

ND - #0196 - 060826 - C0 - 138/138/7 - PB - 9781842890165 - Matt Lamination